Wrapped Up in Life
with Omniscient Eyes
10th Anniversary Edition

Sandra Proto

New York

Published by Amazon Kindle Direct Publishing

Wrapped Up in Life with Omniscient Eyes 10th Anniversary Edition
By Sandra Proto
2nd Edition
ISBN: 9798731842693

Printed in the United States
Cover & Layout Design by Sandra Proto

Dedicated
To my grandmothers Leila Cann and Alberta "Mu" Mims

A Note to Readers

I first published *Wrapped Up in Life with Omniscient Eyes* in April of 2011. The collection consisted of poems that I wrote between twelve and forty (most notable Blackberry Beauty, which I wrote at age 12). During this time, I had little formal training in poetry; in fact, the only training I had was with Tina Chang for a 6-week poetry workshop called Flesh and The Spirit at The Poet's House in 2005. I created several poems, Meditation, Fatherless Children, Possessions, and Our Last Night (In memory of my sister Alberta) in this workshop. The poetic form I used was Free form except for Fatherless Children, a Sestina, and Our Last Night (In memory of my sister Alberta), which was written originally in letter form (epistolary) reworked as a Free form poem for the first edition of *Wrapped*. Also, we used the Leap, a literary device, which is found in the poem Meditation. Overall, I learned quite a lot about the art of poetry writing from this workshop.

However, after *Wrapped Up in Life with Omniscient Eyes'* initial publication, I took two more poetry workshops: Master Haiku Poetry with Sonia Sanchez, and recently, Japanese Poetry History and Form from Local Gem Press. Each was very informative and enlightened me of what I thought I knew what a Haiku was. In the first edition of *Wrapped Up in Life*, I included three poems: Haiku #1, Haiku #2, and Haiku #3. But they were not Haiku because they didn't fit into the standard Haiku structure. So, I changed the title of these poems in this 10th Anniversary edition. Their names are Sitting in the pews…(Haiku #1), For Shana and James Ian (Haiku #2), and Hangin' with friends… (Haiku #3). Also, in this edition, I have restored Our Last Night *(In memory of my sister Alberta)* to its original form of an epistolary prose poem; and added an additional poem, Albert Green Blues *(A Eulogy)*, a poem that I was asked to write from my dear friend Apryl (the poem Apryl's Song is also included in this edition as well as the original). I consider Apryl a sister and, therefore, Albert, a brother. I was honored and nervous because this was the first time, I was asked to write a eulogy.

One thing about writers, we are constantly evolving in our journey. While writing this note, I read over my writing portfolio that I had to compile for the end of the Flesh and The Spirit Workshop. Not only did my writing portfolio consisted of the drafted poems and their revised counterparts but my final comment about the workshop:

> The composition of this poetry portfolio has given me great insight into how writing poetry does not stop after one sign off on it. The process continues when you see the steps of progression to the final destination. It also shows my growth and potential as a poet/writer.

This was true then, and it is now.

After ten years, some life changes have occurred that have pushed more poems into my memory box. Of course, my daughters have grown into teenagers, so To My Daughters is more reminiscent of their infant/toddler years, and seven months after publication of *Wrapped Up in Life* in 2011, my mother passed away. The Woman with Coils (the poem dedicated to my mother) will always be an image that will always be with me.

With this 10th Anniversary edition *of Wrapped Up in Life with Omniscient Eyes*, I hope readers of the first edition and new readers have an enjoyable experience with this collection.

With warm regards,
Sandra Proto

CONTENTS

As the cool air blows,

And the waves rush to the shore like a relay race,
The sand is calm and untouched like me,
I am at peace with myself, for now,
But, soon the wind will blow harder,
And the waves will be at the finish line,
The sand will arise like a tornado,
Bringing everything with it,
And so I am embodied in the sand,
Wrapped up in the tiny grains of life.

Blackberry Beauty

She has very dark skin.
Some say like a blackberry.
When she enters a room,
All eyes are locked on this intriguing figure.
She walks in her own little grace,
Her head carefully lowered at the floor,
Her steps as delicate and graceful as a swan.
When she speaks,
Her voice is a whisper like a quiet storm.
All eyes fall on this blackberry beauty.
Not because she is beautiful.
Some say, "She is ugly because she is way too dark."
Others say, "She is pretty but too dark."
Blackberry Beauty is scorned.
She is two-tones too dark.
But if she was three-tones too light,
Some would say, "She is ugly because she is a wanna be."
Others would say, "She is pretty but too light."
Blackberry Beauty is torn.
She doesn't know if she is ugly or pretty.
She doesn't know if her very dark skin is the cause of her ugliness
    or if she is just plain ugly.
Blackberry Beauty has all eyes on her.
She slowly raises her head and smiles at the onlookers.
Her walk is still graceful and delicate.
Her voice is still a whisper.
She says, "I am the beautiful Blackberry. I was made to be way too dark because I am
ripe. My beauty comes from my blackberry skin and your ugliness comes from your
unripe ones."

Compositions

I, by myself, compose a song inside my room.
The song has the beat and rhythm of my soul.
All the notes and rests are artistically arranged.
The music is subtle and filled with chaos.
With the soft brass sound of the trumpet,
And the easiness of the saxophone,
The xylophone sneaks in with its whispering suggestions.
I, by myself compose this song because it's different.
It has the immortality of classical,
    Sassiness of jazz,
    Earthiness of the blues,
    And a little inspiration of gospel.
I, by myself, compose this song, by myself,
Because no one can compose this song better than I.

My Strength

My Strength comes from my tears of joy
When I see your smiling face

My Strength comes from my tears of pain
When I look into the twinkle of your eyes

My strength comes from my understanding voice
When I soothe you with my sensitive words

My strength comes from my delicate magical heart
When it breaks, on its own it seems to mend

My Strength comes from my naiveness
Like a child I have unspoken innocence

My Strength comes from my stubbornness
When I'm right, I'm right

My Strength comes from my loneliness
When I sit and write this poem

My Strength comes from my poems
They keep me warm and tell me to go on

Poetic Rhythms

Like a dancer's body floating
through the syncopation sounds:

My poetry floats
through my mind
composing poe-ographic movements
with its smooth words
and universal flair.

My poetry takes me to a serene place,
calming my sometimes unsettled mind.

My poetry then travels down my body,
looking for the scattered notes,
so that it can construct harmonific measures
that shoot from my fingertips
to my pen,
creating poetic rhythms for my notepad.

The Poet

I haven't written in a while
I was too busy trying to please others
That I forgot how to smile
I was too busy doubting myself
   With the negative people, places,
   And thoughts
All in which surrounded me
   And tried to suffocate my voice
But now I'm back
   With my voice intact
And like Lorraine Hansberry
I am young, gifted, and black

The Storyteller

The Storyteller observes the world through unprejudiced eyes.
She sits back and slowly digests: the problems, the unfairness,
the joy, the pain of what she has seen. She sits, contemplating
every situation for a resolution. She ponders about how the story
should be told: either narrative or first person. Should it be a play?
a poem? a short story? a novel ? or essay?

Finally, with her hands positioned on the keyboard and her mind
focused: the Storyteller types the story the way she sees it. And hopes
the world will understand the moral to the story for which she has written.

She was adorned

She was adorned in a white headband
with two bows pressed to her forehead.
A white dress draped over her small frame.
She listened as the musician played his
jazz-blues gospel.
She bopped up and down
feeling the rhythm of Jesus enter her soul.
She released a low alto voice that
reminded me of Nancy Wilson.
She strutted around telling her story
of when she rose that morning.

Sitting in the pews...

Sitting in the pews
Tambourines
jingle and jangle

Voices praising God
and loving Jesus
My body shivers

Blessed Kiss

As I strolled down the path

blowing light gray fog

through the cool wind

letting the mist

sprinkle my face with

loving kisses from God

I knew I was truly blessed

Nocturnal Creatures

It's 1 AM
My body is tired.
My brain is wrecked.

My soul is longing to connect with yours.

As I wait for you outside, my mind drifts
to the quiet conversations we often had.   A smile
invigorates me and gives my body energy.

When you pulled up, your eyes
told me you were glad to see me, but
your body was worn like mine.   I jumped
in the front seat and we traveled the bright streets.

Talking
and
smoking

It's early,
so we stop for a game of pool.

You beat me four out of four games.

You ask for a kiss.

To a Potential Lover

They say opposites attract.
Well, let me tell you:
I am the cold moon on a winters' night.
You are the hot sun on a summers' day.
I am the straight horizon.
You are the fluffy clouds.
I am the downtown homebody.
You are the uptown homeboy.
But, when we meet in midtown:
I am a sentimental girl who understands the hard-edge world.
You're a hard-edge guy who has a sentimental side.
Yes, I say opposites attract.
I am the glass filled with ice.
You are the cool drink inside.

The Kissing Game

Our first kiss

Our mouths were nervously entwined in each other's

Our second kiss

Awakened our souls like blooming roses

Our third kiss

Took us to an exciting dangerous place

That kiss

Took
Us
 d
 o
 w
 n

For Shana and James Ian

let my
moist sweet kisses
drench you

let you
soak in the knowledge
I love you

Cuddle Buddies *(for my husband Robert)*

We laid on my floral couch
Our bodies curved into one
Your arm cushioned my head
And your sweet breath
Caressed my neck
Leaving strawberry kisses
I rubbed through your soft hair
Leaving chamomile calmness to your mind
As our hearts beat to the same rhythm

Secret Lover

Your hair

                                      Your lips

                        was so soft

                                                were so tender

Your smile   made me want more of you.

Youreyeswerelikemagnetsdrawingmeclosetoyou.

                                           strong.   You were what I

wanted

                                                    Only you

                     was

can make me

                                          feel real

         body

Your

                Only you can be my secret lover.

My Man

He's tall dark and handsome
His eyes are dark chocolate brown
His skin is deep mahogany
His hair is black coal
    with the softness and sleekness as silk
His height is like a skyscraper
        beaming down on me
His build is firm and sturdy as a mountain peak
His smile can melt a candle without being lit
His lips are juicy, sweet and tender like a ripe plum
His voice is like a big thunder storm
        that makes me shudder at night
His touch burns like a racing forest fire in the woods
His stare is a hypnotic trance
        that'll put me under at just one glance
His embrace is warm and comforting
        like a fireplace on a cold winters' night

He has all of these qualities
But most important
He is my friend
My lover
And
My man

Why do I feel?

Why do I feel alone
> so distant from others?

Why do I feel unknown
> so invisible like the summer's water?

Why do I feel love
> when I see your unforgettable face?

Why do I feel it's enough
> when you hold me in your arms that'll keep me safe?

when in love

when in love
you're a baby sucking on a bottle
you're a child licking the ice cream
you're the cool breeze on the beach
you are satisfied
you are content

when in love
your body tingles all over
    like catching a chill that goes right to the bone

when in love
your mind escapes you
you become instantly dumb

Wasted Love: The Question

Was my love for you wasted?
Should I have crumbled it up
and tossed it in the wastepaper basket
instead of giving it to you?
My wastepaper basket is actually
a ten-gallon barrel filled to the rim with wasted love.
Should I add the one given to you?
So it may overflow?
Or should I smooth out the creases
and put it away in my diary
to write a poem about you?
Tell me,
was it wasted love?
or
pasted memories?

Wasted Love: The Answer

Your love was not wasted.
I just hesitated
'cause I was afraid to love.
Your love fit me too tight
like a child's glove.
Not that your love was overbearing.
But, that a commitment was too daring.
Don't think that I don't care.
'Cause I can feel my heart tear.
Your love was not wasted.
It was me who hesitated.

Could it have been love?

What was it about us being drawn to each other?
What was there?

Could it have been love?

I remembered how when we met
You would always ask for my number
  (and I pretended not to hear you)
We played "catch me if you can" for awhile
Then I finally gave in
  (you called me that same night)

Could it have been love?

Our first date
We were surrounded by friends
Our first kiss
You said was "The best"
  (but the second one was better)
The first time we made love
We brought 1992 in together

Could it have been love?

As we spent more time together
I found out we disagreed with more than a kiss

You wanted me to be something I was not
I wanted you to be something you were not

Could it have been love?

You didn't like the way I
Dressed
Talked
Or wore make-up
But, you didn't listen to what I was saying,
"I have a choice to do or wear what I want"
  (you saw this as disrespect)
I didn't like your "Street Life"
But I accepted it

Could it have been love?

We used to break up
Get back together
Break up
Get back together
This lasted five years
Same old bullshit different year

It couldn't have been love.

If I Apologize

If I apologize

I deny all my beliefs

I deny that I'm an individual

An individual who has

her own mind

her own style

her own way of living

If I apologize

I admit that you were right

But, how can you be right?

This is my life--not yours

I'm the only one who knows myself

inside and out

I cannot apologize

The Dismissal

I was so selfish

I dismissed your pain

I was so stubborn

I dismissed your reason

I had so much anger

I dismissed your love

Meditation

The warm crisp air bellowed through
the window as the bus sped down the highway.

Your face flashed in my mind:
Cold and plaster white.
Your eyes warm moist soil.

The sky was lavender.

My face stared at the omniscient sun
that appeared in the middle of the iron frame
of the Marine Parkway Bridge.
My mind suspended in the uncertainty of our love.

The sky has turned plum-purple.
And the sun has lost its lore.

I stared into my own face.

My eyes ignited its own rhythm.

I sat in my own fire,
cross-legged with palms up.

The moon has brightened up the tar black sky.

You know it's over

You know it's over

When all you can see
  Is the hate in each other's eyes
When all you can feel
  Is the coldness from each other's body from three feet away
When all you can hear
  Is your own heartbeat beating at its normal pace
When all you can taste
  Is your own breath
When all you can think about
  Is "The Affair" that should never had happened
When all you can have
  Are memories
You know it's over

Losing the spirit

Her silver gray hair droops at her shoulders
Her blue and white striped gown masks her frail body
She looks out the window
She sees her past float by in the lucid sky
She sees her future in a tiny brick building
Her eyes grow tired
Her mind grows sad
Her spirit floats away

Our Last Night *(In memory of my sister Alberta)*

Dear Berta,

     As you laid in your pain (that were hot iron spokes jabbing your joints).I rubbed your kneecaps. My warm touch could not surpass your discomfort. My heart shattered into dull crystal shards. *There was a war inside of you.* You cried out for your medication. The morphine patches did not work. You needed your shot of Demerol. *They shoot horses don't they?* Your usual neatly curled hair was disheveled. The nurse suggested that I comb it. I climbed into bed with you and knelt behind you. I brushed and combed through your tarnished hair and made a part down the middle; a bitter sour smell rose up my nostrils. It was a familiar odor (the odor of my own hair when it needed washing). You sat still as I cornrowed two Scarlet O'Hara plaits on either side of your head. *The war had seemed to cease.* When I was finished, I took my green ponytail holder from my hair and married the two ends of your braids. You handed me your favorite scarf (the one imprinted with all of the countries' flags).I tied the scarf around your head. You turned to me and smiled. It was a smile that I had never seen before. My eyes locked with yours and the crystal shards fused with one another making my heart whole again.

     My medicine lasted a little while; then the war began again. The nurse came into your room to administer your shot. You told her where you wanted it. She forcefully stabbed your right thigh. You did not cry but laid there with your eyes closed. *Waiting on relief.* I walked over to you and kissed your moist warm forehead. I then sat down and opened up my book, "A Song Flung Up to Heaven." I peered over a page and heard your brown eyes say good-bye.

     I love and miss you.

Love,
Sandman

My Left Ovary

As you slowly deteriorated
from the cyst that entombed you.
I felt no pain.
A teardrop never flowed from my eyes.
I couldn't understand why
I did not have sorrow.
After all, you held my babies in your sac.
Perhaps, the numbness I still was feeling
from the death of my sister left me apathetic.

But, six months after your passing;
one of my babies from your twin commenced to breathe.
I rejoiced in the coming of motherhood.

Three years and two children later,
I lay caressing my left side
feeling misery invade and replete me.

To My Daughters

Alberta

A smile illuminates my face when I watch you
tottering around:
feet stomping,
head swaying,
waddling like a mother duck leading her ducklings.
You have the spirit of your great grandmother
and aunt—your namesake.

Nicole

My tired arms hold you at 1am…
…and again at 3am…
…and again at 5am…
I gently rub your back, buttocks, and legs
as you suckle at my breast.
I lean my head back (enjoying the silence).
I imagine I am the stream of milk
flowing through your inviting mouth.

Both of you

After nine months of co-existence,
you both were snatched from my womb.

One a week late.

One a week early.

I want back the queasiness
I want back the turbulence
I want back the firestorm
that envelop me
like a lover's embrace.

I am lonely without you.

under the sand's surface

under the dry sun-bleached tan sand lives:
rich-moist nurturing cocoa.
this malleable brown mass
has been kept at bay.
but, soon the rumbling will start
and the volcano will erupt.
spewing cocoa bean raindrops
that fall on the beach
fertilizing the barren land.

Where have all my people gone?

Where have all my people gone?
  With their spiritual songs
Where did they go?
  Somewhere dark and low
Where are they sleeping?
  In cardboard boxes that are leaking
Where are they eating?
  In trash cans with their stomachs beating
Where can I find them?
  Behind the pipe humming its hymn
How can they be helped?
  Stop thinking about yourself

White-eyed Monster

The White-Eyed Monster made the mother kill her child
It tossed the baby from the roof onto the ground
It murdered a young innocent man
It made this earth a Zombieland
It made a young girl become a whore
With two dollars she can score
It destroys hopes and dreams
And it makes a person's body boney and attitude mean
It can make you steal and lie
And it can make your property say good-bye
It can make your family lose their trust
And it can turn your brain into dust
It can make you lose your job and home
And it can make you be all alone

Fatherless Children

The son of the preacher man was parked in front of the playground.
Listening to music and talking to his children.
A young man approached and didn't say a word.
His small black gun made conversation, POP—POP—POP—POP—POP!
The son of the preacher man boys were shocked by what they saw;
 could not believe what happened before their eyes.

A sharp pain rolled up from their stomachs and pierced their eyes.
This was not a game in the playground.
But, reality that cuts jagged like a rusty saw.
The fear of the label, "Fatherless Children,"
produced screams from their mouths, "POP! POP! POP! POP! POP!"
The son of the preacher man slumped over and couldn't hear a word.

They shook and shook him repeating one word,
"OHMYGOD!" as tears smothered their eyes.
A crowd of kids watched, blowing rainbow bubbles, PopPopPopPopPop.
They stood still in the deserted playground.
Parents rushed to their statuesque children
and questioned them about what they had saw.

The kids turned to their parents and stuttered, "I s...s...saw..."
The parents looked in their faces and said, "We all need to hear God's word."
They formed a circle and one parent said, "Let us pray, children."
Everyone bowed their heads with obedient eyes.
The Parents uttered scriptures about the devil's playground
 to an overture of firecrackers: POP—POP—POP—POP—POP!

The speeding car muffler cried: pop...pop...pop...pop...pop.
The elder son driving couldn't believe what they saw.
He regretted meeting his father at the playground.
His brother sat silent not breathing a word.
Sadness spoke through his translucent eyes.
He knew they were brandished "Fatherless Children".

The boys ran into the hospital, a nurse yelled, "What's the matter, children?"
The elder boy spurted out, "It's my Pop...Pop...Pop...Pop...Pop!
The nurse noticed a familiar fear in their eyes.
She could imagine what they had saw.
She looked at them. Her gaze: an unspoken word.
The elder boy said, "He was shot by the playground."

The nurse said, "The Playground!   Anyone else hurt, children?"
The younger boy finally whimpered a word, "Pop, Pop, Pop, Pop, Pop."
The nurse sighed as the younger boy rubbed his eyes.

Lonely Child

The lonely child is hidden in our rooms,
Tucked away behind cloth and paint,
Sheltered from the rest of the house,

No one knows the lonely child.

The lonely child is omnipotent to us,
And insignificant to them,

No one knows the lonely child.

The lonely child is released from our rooms,
We are happy.
We are sad.

We all know the lonely child.

Possessions

Four years dead my husband been
from the pale white disease
that I inherited.
When death stole him away from me:
by law, all of his possessions
belonged to his family.

As death creeps up my bed
the river of pain
is not mine.

Soon Flora will be a mother.
Something that I wished her not to be.
But a mother must forgive her disobedient child
while she is still with the talking.

The only thing I can do with the thin breath
in my weak infectious decaying body
is to order her to eat.

I look at Flora's face
filled with the hills of youth
and her red clay moist eyes hardening.
Her body still has the strength of a girl-child.

But soon the tiny hills will disappear.
And her face will become wrinkled parchment

with encarnado beads protruding from the creases.
Her body will sag like a dying elephant at the sea line.

I have left her this house,
two chairs, and a wardrobe.
I do not regret keeping these possessions
that did not belong to me.

We must fight

We must fight to the end.
Don't let no one box us in.
We have come a long way.
Don't worry:
we'll have our day._
We are a people with the strength of God.
And only to Him shall we nod.

Words

Words
> can cause tears to flow from a lover's eyes

Words
> can cause pain from our spiteful mouths

Words
> can cause hate from our ignorant minds

Words

> Words

> Words

> What are words?

Merely the innocent letters in the alphabet put together to form a weapon
which we call

com   mu   ni   ca
tion

Gay Pride: The Men *(In memory of John "Ms. Rae" Alexander)*

Pay no attention to those
Insecure women and men
Who mock and badger you
They haven't been where you've been

Go ahead
And strut down the street
I'm comfortable about being a woman
So I don't need to compete

Put your
rouge and Donna Karen on
And sing your <Snap!   Snap!>
"Damn, I look good!" song

Be proud of who you are
You know very well
You're a unique star

Gay Pride: The Women

Sister
I may not flow with you
But, I give you respect
And the credit that's due
Unity and love among women
Leaves a tart taste in people's mouths
They are foolish
And in an ignorant-minded group
Who don't understand
What's the real scoop

To a Rapist from His Victim

You came into my life
I didn't want you there
But, you came anyway
Because you didn't care
You came and disturbed my calmness
You came and violated my soul
You came with force and struggle
You came with a deviant goal
You came and destroyed my strength
You came and I lost my trust
You came and my whole world crumbled
   And crumbled into dust
You came and revealed my fears
You came and mutilated my mind
You came and all I could do was say why? Why? Why?
You came and gave no answer
You came and took my life

One year later
One million years beyond
I'm still crying why? Why? Why?

Corporate America

Attaché Cases
Robot Faces
Designer Suits
Lots of Loot
Limousines
And the Beauty Queens
Work Overtime
White-Collar Crime
Kiss Some Ass
Get More Cash
Sleep Around
Your Job Is Sound

Go with the flow
    or you have to go

Omniscient Eyes

Ever see a promotion pass by you
Because you weren't the right shade or hue?

Ever see a man on a disability line
Because he had a fight that made him legally blind?

Ever see a sixteen-year-old girl push a baby stroller
And had another child on her shoulder?

Ever see a grown man cry
When his wife of fifty years suddenly die?

Ever see a mother shout out with glee
When her son's killer enters a guilty plea?

Ever see a child look so confused
Because he doesn't understand why he's being abused?

Ever see a whole family walking down the street
Begging for anything to eat?

Ever see a pregnant woman lose her child
Because her lifestyle was too damn wild?

Ever see a husband hit his wife
The blow was so hard that it ended her life?

Ever see an addict who needed a fix
So desperate that he starts to turn tricks?

Ever see a woman forcibly raped
It may have been your hands that she tried to escape?

Ever see a calm man suddenly snap
And end up at Riker's for a murder rap?

Ever see the world through omniscient eyes?
If you haven't, stop telling lies.

Light

Everything I feel is black and white
Everything I hear is black and white
Everything I taste is black and white
    except for the bright light that falls from the sky
You see, that light is just right
And if you can't see it
All the children in the world are going to breakdown and cry
All the children in the world are going to die
And I'm asking you
Why?
Why do we see black and white?
Why can't we just see the light?

Childhood *(for Lorena)*

Remember when I was eleven and you were twelve
We both were so unsure of ourselves

Remember how close we were back then
Everyone thought we were kin

Remember our nicknames that we had
Owl and Crunchy, the two comrades

Remember how much we both liked to eat
You could tell by lookin' at our fat feet

Remember back then we had so much fun
Playin' hard in the soccer tournament that we almost won

Remember roller-skatin' down your block
And all the teacher's that we mocked

Remember the summer we went to Six Flag's
Finally relieved of our two-ton book bags

Remember the times in Junior High
And all the precious binds that tie

Oh, what a memory I have of you *(In memory of my father)*

1
Your friends and the rest of the family called you
Junior, Junebug, June.
But, I called you dad.
Oh! What a memory I have of you.
2
I think about our last Chicago excursion.
Your CB name was Country Kid.
Remember how you and your brother Big Al skid
down the asphalt road.
Who would make the longest skid mark in town?
You two argued each other down.
Both of you not giving in
'cause you both wanted to win.
And us kids stood enjoying the fun.
We didn't care who really had won.
3
When I think about that time,
my mind envisions all the cars you had.
The red convertible was bad.
The panel-brown station wagon was okay.
And the puke-green Thunderbird had its day.
4
When you took us for a spin
  and swerved smoothly around the bend.
  It was like sailing.
  I held onto the back door like a railing.

  Looking out at the sea of faces.
  Enjoying the differences of the races.
5
You were the Mechanic King.
The way you fixed cars to make them sing.
The smell of motor oil on your navy jumpsuit.
That fit you like a three-piece suit.
Soiled-black hands cradling your tools.
You could have taught at all the vocational schools.
6
Oh! What a memory I have of you.
They make me happy and never blue

Brown young bodies *(naked from the waist up)*

Brown young bodies
(naked from the waist up)
scuttle around
dodging colorful balloons
filled with water

The splatter of the balloons
hitting the cement ground
produced giggles that squirted
out of innocent mouths
A voice from the distance
tells them they can not play there

Brown young bodies
(naked from the waist up)
scuttle around
to find another battlefield

Knowing You *(In memory of my grandmothers)*

I may not have all your years
But, I have your soul
I may not have all your tears
But, I understand your quiet moan
I may not have all your strength
But, I have your backbone
I may not have your ageless beauty
But, I have my own
I may not have your sense
But, I understand it's because you're grown
I may not have what you got
But, knowing you means a lot

The Woman with Coils *(In memory of my mother)*

She sits upright Indian-style on her bed.
Her brown eyes are focused on a murder mystery.
An occasional snap is heard as she
   gently smacks on a piece of gum.
Her well-manicured-berry-tipped hands
 busy themselves:
 twisting
 black-silver-gray curls
 around
 a yellow-mesh roller.
She picks up a plastic baby-pink stick
and expertly pushes it through the netted coil.
She lowers her arms,
enticed by the action that is played before her.

Lady on a Lawka *(In memory of Camilla)*

She is dressed in a valentine-red moo moo,
Her straw-woven chapeau flaps down
    half-covering her face.
Her wide-rimmed glasses firmly
    placed on the ridge of her nose.
The white light obtrudes from the sun,
    as the mild wind skips across her heart-shaped back.
She sits quietly, listening
    to the seagulls banter
    and the rhythmic waves smack across the shoreline.

Friendship

My friends are there to support me.
Not taunt me
or
haunt me.
They're not jealous
or
hellish.
But relish in my company
and I do the same with them too.
My friendship is not based on
"What can you do for me?"
If you think so
You really don't have a clue.
Now you're making me sound like a Who
from Dr. Seuss
going boo hoo hoo.

My friends are my sista,
my brotha
my lova
my cova
on a chilly night.
They're my shoulder,
my boulder,
some are older;
they were sent from the beholder.

My friends never neglect,
always respect,
and come correct.

Apryl's Song

One of my friends was raised in the projects of Sheepshead Bay.
You couldn't tell by lookin' at her
the way her long mousey-brown hair lay.
Outlining her medium frame
flowin' passed her shoulders.
Apryl is her name.
She's my Jewish Sista.
Who always shows "Sista Love."
There's no shame in her game.

The Airbrush Artist *(for Tone One)*

He's an Airbrush Artist.
Don't mistake him for a mere peddler.
He is an artist.
In every sense of the word.

He sells his artwork for a living.
He'll airbrush anything your heart desires.
It could be your favorite recording artist,
A self-portrait,
Or
Your name.
With a steady hand gripping
his fingers around an airbrush tool:
He'll create his artwork on your
Tee shirt,
Jeans,
Jacket;
even your new Nike sneakers.
Not only is he an artist, but
a businessman;
Who knows his self-worth.
He is adamant about his prices.
But can show pliancy when he gives a break
because he knows it will come back to him
tenfold.

The Airbrush Artist finishes his last

masterpiece for the day
and decides to close his gallery
until tomorrow's exhibit.

Hangin' with friends...

Hangin' with friends
Listenin' to the band's techno-pop sounds
Sippin' back Seabreezes

The Music Man *(for my brother James)*

In the room lives an equalizer
co-existing with a DVD player,
which are both placed above a 25" television.
Crates and boxes of tapes, CD's, DVD's, and 33" vinyl records
are standing up against three walls.

The fourth wall,
has a black futon lounging with a small wooden table in front of it.
To keep them company,
a long rectangular green rug is spread across the cool hard white-tiled floor,
warming and cushioning the table's feet.

In the corner,
sits the Music Man surrounded by his instruments:
a soundboard and electronic drum machine
lay flat between stacked-black milk crates,
a keyboard resting on top of a computer cart,
an echo-chamber, compressor, and computer
occupying the shelves.
His ears are covered with muff-like headphones.
His fingers dance around gray buttons on the drum machine.
He swiftly rises and strikes several keys on the keyboard,
changing and composing his beat.
He bobs his head to the orchestrated rhythms.
He is immersed in his creation.

Ray's Rhapsody *(for Ray Charles)*

What do you get when you mix?
      ½ cup of Rhythm & Blues
      ½ cup of Country
      ½ cup of Gospel
1 pound of perseverance
2 pounds of God's Gift
-stir it together on black and white keys.
 Serve it hot in a soulful raspy voice

The end dish: Ray's Rhapsody

Albert Green Blues *(A Eulogy)*

Come a little closer!

To hear the news

I'm gonna tell you
A thing or two
About my brother
It's called
Albert Green Blues!

He was born
July the 28th
Forty-eight years later
He fell in a lake

SPEAK: at Camp Wah-nee; Torrington, Connecticut, to be exact.
It was during a thunderstorm, as a matter of fact. His boat cap side
and the Camp Counselors gave him a ride.   So, Albert jet-skied to the shore.   Well, it
was more like they pulled him along the way. I'll tell you that Albert was never a bore.

Now his Sista' Apryl
And Brotha-In-Law Jan
Can tell you that Albert
Was a big-time fan

SPEAK: of the Beatles, Buddy Guy, James Cotton, Eric Clapton, BB King, and
Cream.
I wonder if he sang to Elizabeth, "I Wanna Hold Your Hand" so you can be my
Queen!

Therein lies
The explicable truth
as James and Emily sit here as proo-oof!

SPEAK: There's a little bit more I have to say about my brother from another
mother.

He played guitar
With local bands

SPEAK: (whisper) Psst…He played Santa Claus
In Macy's Santaland

  He was a gentle giant
  who roared like a lion!

Well…that's what Leos do-ooh

He smiled like a Cheshire cat
and wore his cap like a Top Hat!

Well…that's what Leos do-ooh!

He loved little Mason
his grandson that's two
He was an Uncle and a son
And a father, who had fun too!

He was my brother and friend
Now, my song comes to an end

Well…that was Albert Green Blu-ues!

August 22, 2004:   A Sunday Afternoon

August 22, 2004, on a Sunday afternoon,
I was in Empire Fulton Ferry State Park
taking a break from my volunteer work
for African Voice's Rhymes, Rhythms, and Rituals event.
I walked across the tamed green blades of grass
and stood three feet away from the flat-black stage; waiting
in anticipation for Louis Reyes Rivera and The Jazzoets.
The emcee suggested that Louis introduce the band.
Louis Reyes Rivera, decked in a pinstriped
turquoise black dashiki and baggy white dockers
(I, myself was dressed in a white cotton jersey and
turquoise over-all skirt).
Louis clutched the mic and introduced the multi-
talented performers of The Jazzoets
In his raspy voice that did not seem to fit his petite physique,
Louis said, "Almed Abdullah, the bandleader/composer, is on trumpet.
Atiba Kwabena Wilson, the storyteller, is on flute and percussion.
Ngoma, the poet, is on violin.
And Radu, the composer, is on bass."
The warm breeze rolled down my body rippling my skirt as I squatted
listening to the progressive silky sounds flourish and flirt
from the instruments of The Jazzoets.
Louis took command of the mic.
He was slow and precise with the timing of the music.
Louis Reyes Rivera and The Jazzoets were

    Jammin'
                And
                              Scattin'

    Improvisin'
                And
                              Be-bopin'

Louis Reyes Rivera and The Jazzoets
awakened the drowsy artist in me.

They Came to the Park *(A Salute to the Function at the Junction)*

They came to the park when the sun arose
Families flocking inside the entrance
With legs movin' to the music
Bicycles rollin'
Wheelchairs racin'
Strollers strollin'

They came to the park
Seekin' unity

What they saw were
Blue, green, and pink bubbles shootin' from
Plastic yellow elephants ridin' on the wind
Trees hoverin' overhead blockin'
The glarin' sun from the clear sky
Brown, tan, and even peach bodies
Standin' conversin'
Sittin' relaxin'
Runnin'
Skippin'
Jumpin' double dutch
Playin'
Basketball
Tennis
And
Tag
Coolin' themselves under sprinklers
Even Tweety bird and Spiderman were there
Attached to poles waitin' to go to a child's bedroom

They came to the park
And found unity

In each other's
Eyes
Smiles
Laughter
Joy
And even in the food that they prepared

They came to the park
And they stayed until the sun went down

Observations

1.
Peach bodies sprawled across green hills and pastures
Soaking in sunrays
That makes them cherry-bronze statues
2.
A dark gray pigeon lands
And walks aimlessly around
His head stretching back and fro
Like Mick Jagger
Before he takes off on another journey
3.
A sailboat glides beneath the fireball sun
Across the warm water
And slips under the Brooklyn Bridge
4.
Passersby walk hand-in-hand
Along the path
Falling in love with every step
5.
Curved backs lean toward
New York Times bestsellers
&
Oprah's Book club selections
6.
A Frisbee lands by the feet of a two-year old
He bends down
&
Falls on his cushioned bottom
His dimpled fingers grasp the purple disc and
He places it in his mouth
Gumming it like a teething ring
7.
A man only clothed in a G-string
Sits meditating
8.
I inhale all that I have seen
And laugh to myself
Enjoying the artistry of life

Acknowledgements

I would like to thank Timothy Aaron-Styles and the Wave Publication of Long Island for first publishing *Blackberry Beauty*, *My Strength*, *when in love*, and *Where have all my people gone,*;   Mark Greenfield and the Faux Real Theatre Company, the Rockaway Artists Alliance, and the guys of Hudson's Hope for giving me a platform to showcase my art; Tina Chang and the members of the Flesh and the Spirit poetry workshop for their positive and useful feedback; my family and friends for their love; and all who have supported me throughout the years. Finally, I thank God for guiding me through all of the journeys that I have taken.   I look forward to many, many more.

Also, for this special 10th Anniversary edition, I want to Thank my new friends and readers, who have supported me and my endeavors (especially Ulla Kjarval.)   Ulla continue with your mission in art and advocacy.

About the Author

Sandra Proto is a poet, fiction writer, playwright, blogger, and an essayist originally from South Jamaica, Queens, and Rockaway. She is the editor of *Move Over World; Mary Is About to Holla! Poems by Mary Overstreet (2012)* and has published three volumes of poetry: a full-length collection, *Wrapped Up in Life with Omniscient Eyes* (2011), and two chapbooks, *Spring's Tepid Breath* (2014) and *Sketches: An Exphrasic Journey* (2016). Sandra is the founder of Girls Read to Write LLC.

Sandra Proto resides in Long Island, New York, with her husband and two daughters. For more information go to www.sandraproto.com

Made in the USA
Middletown, DE
23 September 2023

38902506R00042